AF295283

Turquoise

Linda Rose

Books on Demand GmbH (BoD)
Stureplan 4C
114 35 Stockholm
Sweden

Title: Turquoise
Author: Linda Rose
Illustrations: Original photographs by Linda Rose
Graphic Layout: Linda Rose
Second Edition (International, paperback edition)

Publisher and printing: BoD

Available on Amazon

ISBN: 978-91-7463-937-7

Contact e-mail: linda.rose.turquoise@gmail.com

Contents

List of original photographs

Love is Lord

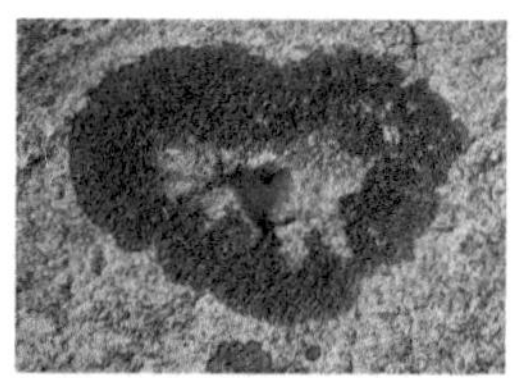

Naturally

My goal

෨෴෩

And my goal:
Love.
Not to conquer,
grasp or capture,
but to
radiate and give.
To share...

෨෴෩

Life and Science on a Sunday

Stillness reigns

Sunday morning
during the sitting practice,
quieting the storms
detaching small-stuff,
rooming the whole;
for a fraction of infinity
stillness reigns.

Insights

Later, indoors,
surrounded by hundreds,
among eager visitors,
in a cacophony
almost overwhelming
I read the nouns,
and poetic words
forming scientific messages.

The inner tranquillity and clearness take me by
surprise
as the insights appear,
as I sense the connections
and try to document them on a wrinkled receipt.

Cosmic rays

You can't see them,
you can't feel them,
but cloud chambers reveal them,
their paths and existence:
the cosmic rays.

Cosmic rays travel faster than our imagination.
A single particle can trigger a chain reaction
sending billions of tinier ones hurtling to earth.

No wonder I sense a hurricane
when hitting ground here
partly in the past
definitely in the present
certainly laying the grounds for the future.

Stardust

Stars and planets form
from the same cloud of gas and dust.
Those rich in certain aspects are most likely to harbour
planets.
- What about us humans?

The life-giving sun's spectrum contains dark lines
- countable in hundreds
showing traces of particles in its atmosphere.
Thus, the particles,
as well as we all, atoms,
leave fingerprints,
each atom absorbing light at a certain wavelength.
-What happens when ours coincide?
- And when they don't?

☙❧

Love

The light of every star
contains a code
telling its story.
What pathways do we take
in our narratives
telling our stories,
making our lives?

Light travels in a straight line
Al-Haitham proved over a millennium ago.
What about love?
What about the reflections in our beloved ones' eyes?
Pure optics?
And the energies,
all parts of the whole?

Heavenly feast

And the rain is pouring down
as if the heavens have opened their wine cellars for a
feast
nourishing all vivid creatures,
with a substance vital for life.
Clearing our vision
- and visions?

৯৩

Relationships

Can we refract our relationships
as easily as we may bend light
when well equipped
with adequate knowledge and tools?

From the same Fountain

We all drink from the same Fountain,
the Science Centre poster stated.
All from the same source.
Some take a precautious sip,
others get drunk just by a sniff
while yet some are bottomless in their thirst.

Love is Lord

In the centre of all
Love is Lord.
However, sometimes it feels so far,
far, far away,
like the galactic centre,
at 28 000 light-years distance.
- How many lonely moon-rounds or reborn lives is that?

෴

Opportunities

'Clouds rest'
in Yosemite,
the glistering surface
on Lake Ontario
and the palette of sun-setting colours above the
treetops
enjoyed from a kitchen with a view,
all give the setting, the opportunities.

Awareness

Gratitude
for the awareness
and the possibility to insight
and to change.

৯০৯

Advantages

If I could stop time now,
would I?
Perchance it would become boring?
Approaching the high amplitude of the sine wave
I must not be at unease or hesitant
but convinced of
the advantages of
awareness, friendship and frankness
and the all-encompassing love.

Love leads the Way

The Great Love
is like a cloud of cosmic rays
with the power to move mountains
and experience from the beginning of time.

A haven,
grey or bright,
in stillness or as a white-water river,
Love leads the way to harbour
like the pan flute and the harp
foreshadow a sense of
and lead to
a heaven.

Love leads the way

Presence

Clean, fresh air,
barren nature.
Nuances come through.
Messengers of contrasts,
contributing to the whole.

It is hard to hear a whisper
in the storm.
In quietness
even the ignorant has a chance
to experience and grasp
the messages
that drown in the jet set stream.

In the rain forest
overwhelming
smells, sounds, spectacular species
attack and numb
our senses and sensitivity.

But in the barren arctic
mountainous quietness
it is easier to note
the beauty in small and large perspectives
and sense the presence
some call God.

Nuances

Night at the base camp

ॐ

The numbness
in my nose
and my limbs
and the chill
when sleeping
in the icy cold
make me so aware
and grateful
for the present
and the presence.

ॐ

At the lakeshore

At the lakeshore
well past dusk
in moonlight.

Carried away,
captured by
the continuum of
water and heavens.

No horizon,
just a continuum of blue
called the universe.
One.

Glistering spring

Drink, drank, drunk...

Drink, drank, drunk...

...

I drink the rays of love and light in nature
as I drank water after a full-day climb in the mountains
and am drunk for the rest of the season
called 'a lifetime'...

In gratitude

&

There's been so much 'life' in my life lately
that I understand the need for rest
and therefore accept and appreciate
these days of bodily illness and exhaustion
enabling reflection in a dark spot
to foster the gratitude and gratefulness
for the rays of love and sun and kindness
falling upon me
this spring,
this year,
this life.

&

Gentle

In the storm
we need to be strong
at core.

Not stiff like a stick,
but supple
as a bamboo plant
still growing.

Aware.
Alert.
Alive.
And gentle.

The rest is silence

☙❧

On this side of the ocean,
in my small world,
there's a full life
with a wide spectrum,
a full sine wave,
'night-and-day' fluctuations,
all present,
all shifting,
constantly.

What we can do
is to be present
to accept what is,
mourn if we have to,
but find comfort in the acceptance
of things we cannot change,
and give our outmost effort for those essentials
that make a difference
in our and in others' lives,
and bring what we call
joy, equanimity and love.

The rest is silence...

☙❧

In an eddy

სტ

Alerts,
alarms
and confusion.

On the other side
Awareness,
quietness
and clearness.

There's a fine line
between tranquillity and chaos.

Some days feel like
confused awakening in an eddy,
abruptly shaken off from sweet dreams
in icy water
with bubbles, noise, currents,
wondering what happened,
where you are,
and where the rescue lies,
what direction to focus the remains of energy on
for a log, a shore, or a saviour.

სტ

Drops of water

Different levels
different nuances
all parts of the same reality.

The heavy, but dancing, bouncing raindrops against my
second skin,
the raingear,
a shield during the quieting time
in the heavy rain;
the glacier water river
streaming with force and strength
rapidly, loudly;
the roaring water masses in the waterfall,
just a couple of stone-throws away...
All come from the same source,
yet appear so different.

−−

The analogies and metaphors to life
seem obvious...

How can there be so much water in the rivers?
How can they float so fiercely,
with such pace,
in spin in forceful eddies?

I can't follow.
Were I to wade further into the river
I'd be dragged along.
Even so, just sitting by the riverside
I realize the fear of
not having the ability to follow,
and of drowning in it all.
Like our lives.

Home

Aspirations of mine

の〜の

Aspirations of mine
are not equal to
expectations of others.
Not even close.

の〜の

I wonder

❧

I've been wondering for some time now...
What do you call it when the candle has
burned down,
burned out,
and the light has ceased to shine?
And what are the meanings of a burn-out?

And the plumed smoke that rises afterwards,
is that part of what makes
stardust?

And stardust;
what kind of entity is stardust?
Is it at all related to cosmic rays?
So many questions,
but no enlightenment.

Any clues,
anyone?

❧

The only way (I)

In tough times
when challenges
seem like a wall
smashingly falling down
I am squeezed.

At states when all demands
feel like
a crazy market
screaming every item out loud
I am drowning.

At places
where expectations
grow to threatening shadows
like chasing arms
I am paralyzed.

When insights and lost capacities
join forces,
giving in
is the only way
not giving up.

The only way (II)

ॐ

When the Sitting,
Metta
and Kata
practices
no longer stand as scaffolding

under the hurricanes
of success,
expectations,
aspirations
and demands,

when sleep starvation
stings all activity
while the storied body
with its pressured chest
and ice-hacked stomach
begs for rest

while burdens
cut off the resilience
and the remaining grains
of coherence
wither away,

ॐ

ੵੵ

when the promised
eternal relationship
with respect
and vowed love
seems lost,

when illnesses,
worries
and caring
for kinsmen
prolong each day,

and low frequency noise
prohibits relaxation;
confusion, chaos
and sadness
move in.

When eventually
the cognitive abilities
malfunction
and the brain
has started shutting down,

giving in
is the only way
not giving up.

ੵੵ

The hardest times

&

The hardest times ever
were not those
bleeding in heart by wounds,
by daggers from the beloved,
and bodkins from worldly matters,
but the emptiness
after,
leaving a vast hole.
Void
past limitations.

&

Air mails

⇦⇨

Air
mails
came.

Tried
decode
cipher.

Will
never
know.

⇦⇨

Diamonds

Diamonds are
said to be
the hardest
of all materials.
Adamantine.

Diamonds are
merely coal
that's been
under hard pressure
for a long time.

Diamonds don't shine,
just reflect
and diffract
others light.

Wanderer's wonders

❧

I wonder
how can all these
everyday people
smile so heartfully,
with such immense warmth?

The moments
my expression is mirrored
in a window or pond
I'm astonished by
the utterly serious look,
further away from a warm smile
than ever.

I sense I should
listen to my heart.
Although so much around me
signals 'yes',
I believe I have to
be true
and bear
to bear
my heart
say 'no'.

❧

Mille colori

Mille colori.
Four o'clock
and the sun
and her brother
befriend each other
across the sky
with an arc of connection.
Displaying a thousand nuances
of colours,
touching a thousand levels
within my soul...

My heart is like a castle

My heart is like a castle
where I find assurance
and rest my soul.

My soul is like a swallow,
at times gliding at low altitude,
foreshadowing rain.

My eyes are like an ocean
often overflowing
purifying all.

November

&ro&

Resting on the moss
focussing on the dew-drops
and the beige-brown blades
of what used to be strong,
intensively green straws of grass,
breathing in the moment

I worship the tiny insect
making its way upwards,
up along this pale path
swaying in the still wind
accompanied by the woodpecker's
hammering picks.

Making its way in quietness,
it strives upwards,
to the highest point
and then
lets go:

gliding,
flying,
brave on its walk of life.

&ro&

❧

In silence
I lie in awe,
in admiration,
and gratitude
to life.

All nuances,
all small signs
of life and its splendour
make me enamoured
even on a grey November day.

Life is not boring,
grey
or hopeless,
not even in November.

❧

What is life?

᷎᷎

If time is a fiction,
what is life?

All in our eye,
all truth or lie

Will we find out
when...

᷎᷎

Spirit free

Wildwood windflowers

Mamma

ॐ

Like a petal in the golden rain
of cherry tree blossoms
in the sunshine.

Now like a seagull,
soars above.
Free.

In the fresh spring day,
in the time of bursting wildwood windflowers,
she has laid down her head
for the last time
in this life.
Spirit free.

ॐ

The Rose

Quietness of sorrow

❦

A gentle sun
softly held by winter clouds
tells the story
of my heart.

❦

Newborn star

∂∞§

The moon is full again
shining so brightly.
I thought it strange
that other night
when new,
yet shining
with such glow.

Before I knew,
it seemed like magic,
yet so familiar
and intense.

Now I know
the shimmer came from a kin,
a new-born star
exploring its first stretch
across the heavens,
warmly radiating love,
hippity-hoppiting with joy,
having joined forces
with the sacred.

∂∞§

The sun

ॐ

And there
in the most difficult of moments
in that strange mixture of
vast emptiness,
extreme presence,
heavy pain, and
previously non-sensed sorrow,
with such grace,
such gentleness,
she glanced through the windows,
showed her face and
then steadily stayed with us
sharing her love,
letting her light
and lightness
fill us.

In the icy stone church,
she warmed my back,
my soul and my heart,
dried my tears,
stilled my grief
and lifted my spirits,
transformed my sorrow into
gratitude and warmth
and love.

And again I sensed
the presence of my kin
as a part
both surrounding and within.

ॐ

The grace of love

లి-ఆ

Later
she made her way again
through the clouds,
gifted us with her warmth,
her view and her love
made me lift my eyes,
my glance and heart
up,
up towards
the skies
the blue
and the heavens.

And while my feet were iced cold,
my tears forming burning drops,
my heart again was lifted
by the gratitude for these moments,
for this life,
and for the grace of love.

లి-ఆ

In a breath

ဆဆ

Seeing his name chiselled in marble today...

In a breath
I'm dismayed
by the definite end,
overwhelmed by the emotion
of missing him,
and empty
as his slippers.

And then
awaken
by the singing birds
to presence,
gratitude,
beauty
and love.

Amazing.
Grace.
All in a breath
in snowfall.

ဆဆ

Angels conspriring

First day

Like the red cup
full of hot strong chai yogi tea
with the label
"Keep true friends close with both hands",
so is the gift of what she gave.

Strong.
Strengthening.
Warm.
Loving.
Like this warm red cup steaming with force.

Warmed.
Filled.
Held.

Just after

భూత

Through bursting nature.
Vivid, like rapture.
In tears.
In endless beauty
and Love.

భూత

Waves

ॐ

Like an escargot carries her home with her
I carry my heart-stone
to remind my stone-heart
of a touch of a scent
of the only thing I used
to live for.

Like the oyster has shot
herself rigidly,
so have I withdrawn into a fortress.
Unreachable.
Shutting off.

As the man in the kayak
focuses on steady, strong, long strokes,
so do I focus
on making a way
in the stormy ocean
called life.

We buried her today
and here I sit
at the oceanfront,
watching the waves roll in
and release into the ocean,
as do our lives.
Some before,
some after.

ॐ

Amazing

☙

It is amazing,
not astonishing,
how the sound of the waves coming to shore,
and the never ceasing pattern of their
coming and going
still my mind
and comfort that,
which some call heart.

☙

Shoulder to shoulder

ॐ∽ॐ

If I could talk to you right now
I'd share my inmost state
in silence.

If I could see you now
I'd share my emotions
and spread some light
through unshielded eyes.

If I could be with you now
I'd sit shoulder to shoulder
sharing my heart
watching the sky.

ॐ∽ॐ

On the vast ocean beach

ঔৰ্ড

On the vast and quiet
ocean tide evening beach
after the storms and floods,
my heart, as the mussel,
held by the sand,
guarded by the heavens,
rests
wide open.

ঔৰ্ড

The mussel

Tonight

❦❧

Tonight world class poetry was on stage in a worn,
leaking café
filled with passion for the spoken word,
with a quivering atmosphere,
and care and love of its poets.

And we stopped breathing,
moved in our inner rooms,
swept off our feet by the truth and beauty,
by their spoken words,
sensing the meaning of your name;
the Perfume of the Fountain of Heaven.

You would have loved it, I believe.
And, yes, I did.

❦❧

Aircraft morning prayer

֍

Time,
my today,
your tomorrow,
what, where, when am I being?

Just here,
just now,
wherever that is,
whenever that is
I pray I'm attuned
to the core
and to the rest
of that vast void...

֍

Friend

When your eyes express sadness or
mirror part of the suffering your soul is going through
they seem to express a concentrate of the sorrows of
this world.
Then I want to be there for you
until the stormy waves have ridden to shore and
quieted,
and be a friend you can share your path with
and a shoulder to lean on when needed.

And then, again,
when your eyes sparkle with joy,
spreading your warmth…
Has anyone ever told you about the effect of your
smiling eyes,
sparkling with joie de vivre
and the radiating Great Love,
has on us,
who have the fortune to be near you?

You lift my soul.

Metta

ॐ

May you be well in every possible way,
May you be joyful and seriously happy,
May you be confident, free from fear, safe,
May you feel loved, and may your heart be open
and deeply peaceful.

May you walk with ease and grace
And may your path be guided by truth and beauty
With purity as wildwood windflowers,
With joyous hope like small spring mountain streams
And clarity as the blue vast void.

May you stay warmly amazing
All days,
All ways,
Always.

ॐ

A lone café

Passing time at a lone café
with a sorrowful friend
is very close to life
- as close as you can get.

Storied heart

Futurespective

I have a friend
I feel whole with.

When gone
the letters will
bestow harmony.

When gone
the memories will
remain with warmth.

When gone
the endless and boundless
will radiate:
Love.

Reflections at the train station

The skies above,
the clouds moving in different directions,
some slowly, some rapidly,
some approaching each other,
others slowly gliding apart
- at different levels
just like we...

Taking this in as all truth and beauty
while a high speed train roars by,
awakening me to another part of the presence
here and now,
at ground level.

And the quivering leaves on the trees
dance in their new red dresses
in the fresh autumn breeze.
Just like we...

Alive, alive, alive...

In the morning light

The morning light,
the stillness around,
make me stop.
Or perhaps it's just the perception
of time and love and light
that is altered for a while.

In the hour of blue
everything is possible.

Perchance sleep also.

A blade of grass

Dewdrops

Conspiring (breathing together)

Being here

෧ஐ

Being here,
being sensitive and open
to the small, sometimes subtle, signs
that can foster, nourish
gratefulness and love.

It may lead the way
like wood anemones
border the forest trail,
guiding our zig-zag path in life.
All days.

෧ஐ

Wood anemones

In the hour of blue

৵৹৶

In that moment
when night and day
in trust, respect and presence
do the act of love and beauty
day after day:
embrace,
I just know...

They are not opposites,
nor fulfilling parts,
just different expressions
of what we call
the Whole
and is
All.

৵৹৶

Narsarsuaq

୤௦ீ

Shadows of snow-white clouds
leave the same traces on ground
as lakes
seen from above.

And like the Milky Way
spreads its stars over the sky,
so do the ice blocks
spread in the Arctic Sea
outside Narsarsuaq
off Greenland's coast,
spread like shining stars
on the dark surface.

Amazing.

All
just One...

୤௦ீ

The moon is new tonight

❧

The year is young,
as is the decade.
The moon renewed,
as is my love

for this world
and this life.
Eventful, yes, but calm.
True, beautiful and warm.

❧

My soul is dancing

Again, no words.
As the first signs of light
spread
turning the night into
the hour of blue
I read a poem,
am lost in time
and found in presence.

And my soul is dancing.

Turquoise

On the path
on my way from work
in life
through life
to life
on the saddle
quietly,
but with pace, speed,
feeling extremely alive,
riding against the warm summer-breeze
on the lakeshore
I pass an eggshell,
turquoise
as the colour of hope.

❧

For a second I consider
squeezing the brakes,
stopping,
turning and going back
to immortalize the image
with a snap shot.

Then I realize
it's superfluous.
Forever the shell,
its shape and colour
and their combined meaning
will be with me.

❧

Along the path

Time to get serious

ॐ

In a way,
I'd just like to take off for some time,
get into an undisturbed cave or cottage and
fully enter the state
via an unrestricted channel to the inmost layers of my
soul,
where I can spend some time
being at the core,
and take a step further on my journey.

Maybe coat the inner self in awareness,
expressible feelings, tones or words.
Not joyously sparkling,
not sad,
but essential
and true.

Then again, the big question rises
about what path to prefer,
what path to choose.
I've developed so many models in my job,
but perhaps it's time to get serious.

ॐ

Siblings

☙❧

The ice-blocks off Narsarsuaq's coast
and the stars in the sky
appear alike from distance.

Light-years apart,
so different in essential characteristics,
conditioned by their contexts.

Yet, mere stardust
united and separated
by space.

☙❧

Icebergs

ॐ

Icebergs...
Under pressure and
sustained cold
they turn into glaciers.

Rough, stony, edgy, hard.
Tough and dangerous.

But, in their cracks
they have a shimmer of turquoise,
the colour of hope.

ॐ

The essence

ॐ

Woke up at 'just-to' four
with another of those sentences
striking me awake like a shower,
striking my awareness as a lightning
urging all fibres in my being
to get up and latch onto
the sensation.
Not about regression analysis
or mathematical equations,
but about life.

Tell a table it is a bird
and it might fly;
Tell me I'm poet
and I will continue
waking up in the midst of night
get up
and endeavour to
grasp the sensation
as the turquoise
catches the essence
of hope.

ॐ

To life

☙❧

After the words,
thoughts,
and feelings
have ceased,
a numbness
remains.

But after vacuum,
and the dust to dust,
light to light
trickles from the inmost secret spot,
the treasured hidden storm light.

And as the turquoise ray
makes way as Hope,
so does this Light,
the true sign of the Whole,
find its way
to daylight,
to consciousness
in Life.

☙❧

Towards light

Held

On the bus
in stillness.
And, as the haze gathers all closer
its freshness and softness
make me feel held.
Embraced.

The choice

꙰

When there is a choice
– and I believe there is –
choose love.

꙰